THE MILLIONAIRE

MINDSET

How To Think Like A Millionaire
And Achieve Financial Freedom

O.G. CEO

Photo Credit: iStock Free Images

Cover design by: Art Painter

Library of Congress Control Number: 2018675309

Printed in the United States of America

Dedication

This great and mindset-transforming book is dedicated to everyone who will employ the principles in this book to think like a millionaire and achieve financial freedom.

Table of Contents

Introduction

Here you will learn "How to Think Like a Millionaire and Achieve Financial Freedom" (or "The Millionaire Mindset" for short). This book will teach you how to think like a millionaire to gain independence from the financial worries you've always wanted.

The Millionaire Mindset: What Is It?

The millionaire mindset is a method of thinking whose primary goal is accumulating vast wealth and the consequent freedom from reliance on others. An attitude of plenty, as opposed to one of shortage. This way of thinking emphasizes doing what needs to be done rather than finding reasons not to.

Having a millionaire mentality is not a luxury only the wealthy can afford. That kind of thinking is something that can be learned by everyone, regardless of their financial standing. This way of thinking is something that can be taught and developed with time, effort, and curiosity.

To what extent does it matter that you adopt the mentality of a millionaire?

To reach your financial goals, you need to adopt a millionaire attitude. Financial success is only financially possible with the proper frame of mind. Adopting the millionaire mindset is the secret to realizing your full potential and accomplishing your financial goals.

The antidote to the scarcity mentality that permeates modern culture is the millionaire mentality. The scarcity mentality is one that constantly anticipates and dwells on potential setbacks. It's a mode of thinking that dwells on lack rather than abundance.

The attitude of scarcity is the primary barrier to monetary independence. This is the root cause of why so many individuals cannot make ends meet and why so few people ever become financially secure. The millionaire mentality might help you overcome a lack of resources. In other words, it's the secret to finding success and enjoying the fruits of your labor monetarily.

Exactly what are its takeaways?

This book will teach you the fundamentals of success and the techniques millionaires use. Discover the secrets of the wealthy and start living the life of your dreams today.

What you'll pick up is:

1. The significance of maintaining an optimistic outlook and the necessary steps.
2. Developing a strategy for setting goals that you can and that are in line with your beliefs and long-term vision.
3. Methods for overcoming the self-doubt and self-sabotage that prevent many people from realizing their full financial potential.
4. Methods for maintaining forward motion toward one's monetary objectives and generating the energy necessary for enduring change.

5. Methods for generating and diversifying different sources of income.

6. Long-term wealth management and portfolio diversification are covered.

7. The steps to adopting an attitude of plenty and bringing financial success into your life.

8. Long-term motivation and momentum-building strategies.

This book is not a quick fix to financial problems. This book will show you how to think like a millionaire and lead you to long-term financial security. It's a manual built on tried-and-true methods to bring about long-term prosperity for its reader.

Today's global economy is fraught with perplexing obstacles. It can be challenging to achieve financial success due to rising living costs, rising debt, and uncertain job security. Nonetheless, many overcome and build sustainable sources of wealth and independence. What makes these individuals special? It's fundamental to their way of thinking.

The millionaire mindset is characterized by an outlook that prioritizes plenty above want. Rather than finding reasons not to do something, this mindset encourages doing something about it. Instead of waiting for opportunities to present themselves, this mindset actively seeks them out.

A millionaire's mindset is based on a set of concepts and tactics that we'll examine in this book. The key traits of self-made billionaires that have contributed to their financial success will be dissected and analyzed. We'll also discuss some of the most common barriers to achieving the millionaire mindset, as well as some effective ways to overcome them.

Yet becoming financially secure is only one aspect of establishing a billionaire mentality. Making a happy and successful life for oneself is the goal. To live a life in harmony with your principles and your ultimate goals. It's about making sure you're happy on all levels, not just monetarily.

You can use this book whether you're just getting started with your finances or you're ready to take your wealth-building to the next level. It's a how-to manual for adopting the mentality of a multimillionaire, and it'll help you get there by showing you how to make money and invest it wisely so that you can live the life of your dreams.

Creating a billionaire mentality isn't something that can happen overnight. It calls for persistent work, an open mind, and decisive action. But if you have the correct attitude, you can accomplish anything. You will find yourself well on your way to financial independence and a life of wealth and fulfillment if you follow the tactics and principles presented in this book.

Chapter 1

The Millionaire Mindset: An Overview.

The need of developing a "millionaire's mindset" to get where you want financially is outlined in this section. It gives a quick summary of the fundamental themes discussed throughout the book and describes the contrasts between the millionaires and the average person's perspectives.

* The Importance of a Positive Attitude to Your Success

* Understanding the Value of an Optimistic Perspective and Learning to Foster It

* How Confidence Helps You Succeed in Business.

* The Key to Realizing Your Potential: Overcoming Fear and Self-Limiting Beliefs

Realizing the Influence of Your Attitude

The first step toward creating a millionaire mentality is realizing your thoughts' impact on your success. You can only expect to be financially successful if you first change your perspective because your outlook affects how you deal with every element of your life, including money.

Your money, wealth, and success-oriented frame of mind consist of your beliefs, expectations, and assumptions. Your thoughts and feelings are the driving force behind your actions. How you choose to think about obstacles or opportunities might be the difference between moving forward and staying stagnant.

The core of the millionaire mindset is the conviction that anyone can build wealth so long as they are dedicated to the process and maintain a positive outlook on their financial situation. Thinking like this is not about being impatient or skipping steps. To become financially independent, one must develop a long-term mindset, learn to wait for gratification, and take intelligent risks.

To achieve the level of success associated with the "millionaire mindset," it is crucial to recognize the impact your thoughts and attitudes have on your financial outcomes. Some fundamental guidelines are as follows:

The way you think dictates the way you behave.

What you think determines what you do. If you think making money is unattainable, you won't take the initiatives that could lead to wealth development. Instead, if you adopt a millionaire's mentality, you'll be more likely to pursue opportunities, take calculated risks, and make the required sacrifices to reach your objectives.

What you think about impacts what you see.

What you focus on and how you understand the world are both products of your frame of mind. A pessimistic outlook will have you fixating on all the problems and setbacks that you still need to overcome. On the other hand, if you keep a sunny disposition, you'll give more thought to the prospects and possibilities that lie ahead.

How you think impacts the convictions you hold.

What you think is possible depends on your frame of mind. If you have a narrow perspective on the world, you may think that factors beyond your control predetermine your socioeconomic status. But if you think like a billionaire, you'll know that your success in life is up to you and your effort to improve yourself and your skills.

Your state of mind affects the way you feel.

How you feel and think about money is affected by your thinking. A pessimistic outlook increases the risk of making financially irresponsible choices like putting off necessary expenses or putting off paying down debt. On the other hand, if you keep a positive outlook, you'll have more faith in your abilities and a greater belief in your ability to amass wealth.

In conclusion, your frame of mind is the cornerstone of your monetary success. The first step toward creating a millionaire mentality is realizing the impact your thoughts have on your success. You can reach your full potential and achieve financial freedom by developing a healthy relationship with money, having a long-term view, and making smart risks.

Understanding the Value of an Optimistic Perspective and Learning to Foster It

Having a positive perspective on making annoying money is crucial to developing a millionaire mindset. Because it influences your ideas, feelings, and behaviors, a positive outlook can substantially impact your financial performance. An optimistic outlook increases the likelihood that you will take the initiative, look for chances, and make concessions to reach your objectives. Here, we'll discuss the value of a sunny disposition and offer advice for cultivating one.

How Beneficial an Optimistic Perspective May Be

A millionaire's mindset requires a specific way of thinking about money and wealth, and one's outlook greatly influences that way of thinking. To have a healthy relationship with money, one must see it not as a cause of worry or anxiety but as a means to an end—the life one desire. If you adopt this mindset, you can approach your financial situation with optimism, confidence, and a willingness to take chances.

Having a constructive outlook on wealth creation also aids in overcoming self-doubt and limiting beliefs. It's much easier to take the initiative and keep going when you have faith in your ideas and the possibility of creating wealth.

Create a Better Mood: The Science of Optimism

Whether you've been through financial difficulty or if you have negative ideas about money, it can be not easy to adopt a positive outlook on money and the accumulation of wealth. A positive outlook and constant effort, though, can lead to the kind of success that can set you free financially. Some suggestions for improving one's financial outlook:

Express Your Appreciation and Thankfulness

Having a grateful mindset is one of the simplest ways to change your relationship with money. To do this, you must stop worrying about what you don't have and start appreciating what you do.

An attitude of gratitude can be a powerful strategy for overcoming negative thought patterns because it encourages you to focus on what you have rather than what you lack.

Rethink Your Worldview

Reframing your assumptions about how to amass wealth is another option for improving your financial outlook. Rather than viewing money as a scarce or unattainable commodity, try to view it as a means to an end—a means to the life you want to live. Changing your perspective can help you overcome self-doubt and limiting beliefs, giving you a more optimistic outlook on your financial situation.

Put yourself in a position to succeed by surrounding yourself with good people.

The company you keep can have a major effect on your outlook. Having mentors or friends who are encouraging of your financial objectives can be a great source of inspiration and motivation. As a bonus way of thinking about how to amass riches.

Visualization Exercises

Having a positive mentality toward financial success can be greatly aided by the practice of visualization. Having a mental image of your future financial achievement might help you keep motivated and on track toward your goals. The ability to visualize optimistic outcomes is a powerful tool for maintaining optimism in the face of adversity.

Start Slow

Working towards your financial objectives one step at a time will make you feel better about money. Even incremental strides toward your objectives can serve as a potent source of motivation and encourage you to keep going. To add to the positive feedback loop, taking baby steps might help you gain momentum and confidence.

In conclusion, cultivating a millionaire mindset requires adopting an optimistic outlook on financial success and wealth building. You may change your mindset and work toward financial independence through appreciation, re-frame from negative beliefs, surrounding yourself with good influencers, visualization, and baby steps. Financial success isn't the only thing that can be improved by adopting a positive outlook on life; you can also use it to make your life more abundant and fulfilling.

How Confidence Helps You Succeed in Business

Millionaire mindset traits include a strong sense of self-belief, which is often neglected but crucial to achieving financial success. Faith in one's abilities and the assurance to pursue such abilities constitute self-belief. Fundamental to self-confidence is faith in one's value, potential, and skills. Here, we'll discuss why confidence is so crucial and offer some advice on how to build your own.

Recognizing the Value of Confidence in Oneself

The confidence to push through your limits is crucial to developing a millionaire mindset. Confidence in oneself and one's talents increases the likelihood that one will take action to achieve their goals and keep going despite setbacks. Self-belief allows you to trust your conclusions and judgment, even if others don't.

The ability to overcome obstacles and disappointments is another benefit of having confidence in oneself. If you have faith in yourself, you will be more resilient to setbacks and better able to recover and go on. In addition, you are more inclined to view setbacks as learning experiences rather than evaluations of your value or competence.

Learning to Believe in Yourself

Confidence in one's cities is a trait that takes time and effort to cultivate, especially if one has struggled in the past or holds unfavorable attitudes about oneself. Consistent effort, on the other hand, will help you build the kind of rock-solid confidence that will lead to material success. Here are some suggestions for bolstering your confidence:

Throwing Out Preconceived Ideas

To build confidence in yourself, it's important to question the false ideas you may have about yourself. Some examples of such false notions are "I'm not smart enough" and "I don't have what it takes to be successful." Refuting these false notions will help you develop a more optimistic self-image and a firmer foundation of self-confidence.

Recognize Your sizing and appreciating your qualities and successes is another route to greater assurance in yourself. It's important to think about the attributes that led to your past triumphs. Your self-esteem and sense of competence can both benefit from a healthy dose of positive self-analysis and a concerted effort to highlight your many positive traits.

Identify and spend time with positive influences.

Your sense of confidence can be greatly influenced by the people you keep close to you. The confidence you need to succeed can be bolstered by the presence of positive, encouraging people who have faith in you. When you need it most, these people will be there to give you a boost of confidence, constructive criticism, and unwavering support.

It's important to Aim Reasonably

Having faith in one's abilities also requires setting reasonable expectations for oneself. Having faith in your abilities increases when you aim for goals that are both difficult and doable. If you set your sights too high, you may end up feeling disheartened and disappointed in yourself.

Applaud Your Successes, No Matter How Little

Last but not least, recognizing and appreciating even minor successes can go a long way toward building confidence. It's important to recognize and reward yourself for accomplishing even the smallest of goals along the way if you want to build confidence in your capacity to complete the larger ones. Little successes can go a long way toward keeping you motivated and focused on your larger financial objectives.

In conclusion, confidence in one's abilities is essential to developing a millionaire mindset. Building self-belief is an effective strategy for achieving success in many areas of life, including the financial realm. Self-belief can be nurtured by the systematic elimination of self-limiting ideas, the cultivation of a positive social environment, the establishment of reasonable expectations, and the recognition and celebration of incremental successes. A solid foundation of self-confidence is the key to monetary success and the freedom to design the life you want.

The Key to Realizing Your Potential: Overcoming Fear and Self-Limiting Beliefs

Fear and limiting beliefs might prevent us from reaching our greatest potential. Past events, societal upbringing, and negative self-talk can all contribute to the development of such beliefs and phobias. Here we will discuss methods for overcoming self-doubt and anxiety on the road to realizing one's full potential and monetary success.

Distinguishing Self-Limiting Beliefs

Recognizing self-limiting ideas is the first step toward changing your mind. Negative attitudes and ideas, known as limiting beliefs, prevent us from progressing toward our objectives. Negative self-talk can be triggered by telling yourself things like, "I'm not good enough," "I'm too old/young to reach my goals," or "I don't have enough experience or education to be successful."

Start by monitoring your internal dialogue to unearth limiting beliefs. Recognize when you are talking negatively to yourself or making false assumptions about yourself or the environment around you. Once you become aware of them, you can begin to challenge and replace your limiting beliefs with more positive and empowering ones.

Subverting Confidence-Reducing Ideas

To reach your maximum potential and cultivate a millionaire mindset, it's crucial to question and overcome self-limiting ideas. Questions like "Is this belief true?" or "What evidence do I have to support this view?" can help identify and overcome limiting beliefs.

Consider the limiting notion, "I'm not good enough," and ask yourself if it's true. You may come to see that your erroneous view rests on nothing more solid than your negative thinking or an outdated set of experiences. Then, you can switch to a more positive and empowering mindset, such as "I can study and grow into the person I want to be, and I can accomplish anything I set my mind to."

Reframing limiting beliefs in a more uplifting way is another method for combating them. It's possible, for instance, to reframe the notion that "I'm too old/young to attain my goals" as "I have a unique viewpoint and experience that can help me achieve my goals."

Conquering Fear

Having a millionaire mentality and reaching our maximum potential are both hindered by fear. Some of the most common sources of fear are not knowing what will happen, failing, or being rejected. It can show up as avoidance, procrastination, or uncertainty in one's abilities. But if we face our fears head-on, we can conquer them and reach our full potential.

Exposure therapy is a useful method for conquering phobias. This entails exposing oneself to feared stimuli in little doses, over time, and under supervision. If you suffer from a fear of public speaking, for instance, you can ease into the experience by addressing a small group of people you know well, such as friends and family.

Recasting your fear as a challenge, rather than a danger, is another method for overcoming it. Fear is a normal response to anything that could potentially harm you, but instead of seeing it as a sign of failure, you should see it as a chance to learn and improve. When you adopt a growth mindset, you may overcome your fears, work toward your goals, and become more resilient in the face of adversity.

The ability to conquer your fears and realize your full potential is aided by establishing a self-care practice. Exercising, meditating, keeping a journal, and spending time in nature are all examples of self-care practices. Engaging in these pursuits can aid in stress reduction, enlightenment, and the development of a strong character capable of withstanding danger and adversity.

In conclusion, we might let our lack of confidence and self-doubt prevent us from reaching our goals and becoming financially independent. We can overcome these obstacles and reach our full potential by recognizing and disputing limiting beliefs, engaging in exposure therapy, recasting anxiety as a challenge, and establishing a self-care routine. The road to material prosperity and the fulfillment of our dreams begins with the mastery of our inner critic.

Chapter 2

The effectiveness of an optimistic outlook

The importance of optimistic thinking in creating a millionaire mentality is explored in this chapter. Optimism, the value of problem-solving over problem-fixing, and the potential of mental imagery are all topics covered.

★ Science and the Art of Optimism

★ How an Optimistic Attitude Can
Help You Succeed Financially
★ Tools for Fostering Optimism

Science and the Art of Optimism

The strength of positive thinking is in its ability to aid in the attainment of our goals, the promotion of our health and well-being, and the improvement of our quality of life in general. The research on the effects of optimistic thinking on one's well-being reveals that the way we think and feel can profoundly affect our actions and even our bodies. Here, we'll examine the studies that have been conducted on the topic of positive thinking and its physiological and neurological impacts.

Science and the Art of Optimism

By "positive thinking," we mean the habit of choosing to dwell on positive mental and emotional experiences rather than moping over the bad. Brain regions involved in reward processing, including the prefrontal cortex, amygdala, and hippocampus, are stimulated when we think positively. A person's mood, drive, and memory are all controlled by these regions of the brain.

The amygdala is a tiny almond-shaped structure in the brain's limbic system. In specifically, it handles anxious and fearful feelings. The amygdala becomes less active and our levels of fear and anxiety go down when we think positively.

In contrast, higher-order cognitive processes, including decision-making, problem-solving, and planning occur in the prefrontal cortex. The prefrontal brain becomes more active during optimistic thinking, allowing for more creative thought and improved decision-making.

The hippocampus has a role in learning and memory as well. Researchers have shown that optimists have a larger hippocampus, which improves their memory and learning.

How an Optimistic Attitude Can Help You Succeed Financially

There are several ways in which a positive outlook might help one succeed monetarily. More optimism, motivation, and resilience can be developed through the cultivation of positive mental and emotional states. These traits will be crucial in overcoming obstacles and realizing our financial objectives.

For instance, optimism is the conviction that one can accomplish one's aims despite obstacles. Those that are optimistic are more willing to try new things, seize opportunities, and bounce back from setbacks. Achieving financial success requires adopting this mentality, which helps us keep going even when things get tough.

Success in the financial realm also requires a healthy dose of inspiration. Keeping a positive frame of mind increases our drive to work toward our ambitions. Thinking positively strengthens our sense of purpose and motivation, allowing us to take on new tasks and move closer to realizing our goals.

Having the strength to recover quickly from adversity is an essential quality for success. Positive thinking strengthens our mental fortitude, allowing us to bounce back swiftly from disappointments and keep moving forward in the direction of our dreams. This outlook is vital for obtaining monetary success since it enables us to persevere in the face of adversity and conquer any barriers that may stand in our way.

Tools for Fostering Optimism

Adopting a more optimistic outlook is a process that calls for time and effort.

Here are some methods you might take to train yourself to think more optimistically:

The act of being grateful is one of the most powerful strategies to train oneself to think constructively. When we take time to reflect on all that we have to be thankful for, we can redirect our attention away from the things at may be causing us distress and toward those that are worth celebrating. One way to cultivate an attitude of thankfulness is to keep a gratitude notebook or to set aside time every day to think about what you're grateful for.

Your internal conversation has a huge effect on your frame of mind and mood, therefore it's important to keep it upbeat and encouraging. Reframe negative thoughts into positive ones and practice positive self-talk. Think positive thoughts, like "I am capable of overcoming this problem" instead of "I can't do this."

The practice of visualizing oneself as having already accomplished one's goals is known as visualization and is an effective tool for reaching one's objectives. Visualization has been shown to engage the same brain networks as the real performance of a task.

How an Optimistic Attitude Can Help You Succeed Financially

In the realm of self-improvement, the importance of maintaining an optimistic outlook cannot be emphasized; the same is true when it comes to monetary success. Your success in accumulating wealth depends in no little part on your mental attitude, and this attitude can be shaped by the way you think. In this article, we'll discuss how an optimistic outlook can help you build wealth.

Motivation

Motivating oneself is impossible without an optimistic frame of mind. Concentrating on the bright side of things increases our drive to work toward our goals. The quest for material prosperity requires this kind of constant effort and devotion. With the right frame of mind, nothing can stop us from taking on new challenges and going for our goals.

Optimism

Positivity is the conviction that one can succeed despite obstacles. Those that are optimistic are more willing to try new things, seize opportunities, and bounce back from setbacks. Achieving financial success requires adopting this mentality, which helps us keep going even when things get tough. When we maintain a positive outlook, we are more able to view difficulties as lessons.

Resilience

The ability to recover quickly from difficulties is a hallmark of resilient people. Positivity strengthens the mind, making us better capable of shrugging off challenges and moving forward with our lives. This outlook is vital for obtaining monetary success since it enables us to persevere in the face of adversity and conquer any barriers that may stand in our way.

Creativity

An optimistic outlook improves our capacity for original thought. Positivity allows us to see possibilities where others only see problems. By adopting this perspective, we are better able to think creatively about how to address budgetary issues. Finding new ways to make money and add to one's wealth is crucial to achieving financial success, and here is where one's creative abilities come in.

Greater ability to make choices

Keeping a sunny disposition helps us make wiser choices. We are more likely to make decisions with an open mind and a willingness to take risks when we are feeling optimistic. Thanks to adopting this frame of mind, we are better able to make choices that bring us closer to our financial objectives. The ability to think rationally, examine alternatives, and assess consequences improves when we maintain an optimistic outlook.

Enhanced connections

Relationships benefit from a more optimistic outlook as well. Positivity increases the likelihood that we will form meaningful connections with people who will help us achieve our monetary objectives. The people in our lives can be a tremendous source of both the emotional and material support necessary to help us succeed in our pursuit of financial independence.

A Healthier Life

Think positively, and it can do wonders for your body and mind. Studies have found that keeping a positive outlook can have beneficial effects on one's health, including lowering stress and blood pressure and boosting the immune system. When we're physically and mentally fit, we're better able to work hard for our financial objectives. By lowering stress and despair, which can hinder rational decision-making when it comes to money, positive thinking also improves our physical health.

In conclusion, a positive outlook is a potent resource for expanding our economic opportunities. To reach our financial objectives, we need the drive, optimism, resilience, creativity, and sound judgment that come from adopting a positive mental attitude. Achieving our financial goals is entirely under our control, and we may do it by developing an optimistic outlook.

Tools for Fostering Optimism

Achieving financial success can be facilitated by maintaining an optimistic outlook. The preceding paragraph discussed how an optimistic outlook might help you succeed financially. Here, we'll discuss methods for developing an optimistic outlook.

Express Your Appreciation and Thankfulness

When you train your brain to focus on the good, you train yourself to see the world in a more optimistic light. Positive thinking makes us more appreciative and thankful. The practice of gratitude can help us turn our attention from the unpleasant to the positive parts of our existence. To cultivate an attitude of thankfulness, try spending some time each day thinking about the good things in your life.

Think About Ways Out

An additional effective method for developing a more constructive outlook is to center one's attention on potential avenues for resolution. When we set our sights on resolving a problem or overcoming a hurdle, we increase the odds that we will do so. Keeping our attention on potential avenues for moving forward will help us reorient our thinking away from any lingering unpleasant feelings. To shift your mindset into a solution-focused one, try asking yourself what you can do to fix the issue at hand.

Be in the company of upbeat individuals.

The company of upbeat and optimistic individuals can do wonders for one's outlook. Being around upbeat, optimistic people has a contagious effect. When we surround ourselves with positive individuals, we receive the support and motivation we need to keep pushing forward toward our goals. To maintain a happy mental state, it is important to spend time with supportive people regularly twice upbeat self-talk

Positivity can also be cultivated through another powerful tool: positive self-talk. More confidence in our skills and hope for the future can be attained through positive self-talk. By focusing on the positive aspects of our lives and refocusing our attention away from the negative ones, we can overcome our tendency to dwell on the latter. Refraining from negative self-talk entails refocusing one's attention on one's positive traits and successes.

Focus on Achieving Your Goals

Successful people often use mental imagery as a means of strengthening their optimistic outlook. Positive self-image and confidence in one's abilities are cultivated via the practice of mental imagery. By creating a mental image of achieving our goals, we are better able to replace negative self-talk with optimistic anticipation of our desired results. Take some time every day to imagine yourself having achieved your financial objectives and living the life of your dreams.

Do some Mindfulness Training

Mindfulness practice is yet another potent method for developing an optimistic outlook. Mindfulness training improves mental health by making us more self-aware and thus more capable of controlling negative emotions and distracting thoughts. By bringing our attention to the here and now, mindfulness helps us disengage from destructive mental patterns. Mindfulness entails paying attention to one's internal experiences, such as one's thoughts and feelings, without attaching any value judgments to either.

Pay Attention to Your Development

An additional potent method for developing a more optimistic outlook is to concentrate on one's elopement. When we put our attention on developing ourselves, we gain faith in our abilities and hope for the future. When we work on ourselves, we can change our focus from the negative to the positive, where we can see our true potential for growth and development. Establishing and working on personal goals is an effective way to concentrate on development.

In sum, developing an optimistic outlook is an effective strategy for reaching one's financial goals. A positive mentality can aid you in reaching your financial objectives if you nurture it through activities like thankfulness, focusing on solutions, surrounding yourself with positive people, engaging in positive self-talk, envisioning achievement, practicing mindfulness, and focusing on personal development. If you can keep a positive outlook on life, you'll be more likely to take charge, stay the course, face setbacks with grace, come up with novel solutions to problems, and make wise choices with your money.

Chapter 3

Successful Goal-Setting Strategy

In this chapter, you'll get advice on how to create meaningful, long-term objectives that are within reach. It discusses the value of SMART objectives (targets that are specific, measurable, attainable, relevant, and time-bound) and offers concrete advice for cultivating a goal-oriented outlook.

- ★ Motivating Yourself to Achieve Financial Achievement Via Goal-Setting
- ★ Learn the Secrets of Financial Success by Establishing SMART Objectives
- ★ Effective Methods for Reaching Your Financial Objectives

To Achieve Monetary Success, it is Crucial to Set Goals.

Establishing and sticking to goals is crucial to gaining financial independence.

Without defined objectives makes it is tough to take the necessary actions and evaluate success. Here we'll talk about the value of planning for the future financially.

Gives One Direction and Emphasis

Making a plan for your money helps you focus and direct your efforts. Setting goals can help you see more clearly what it is you desire and the path you need to take to get there. They assist you to plan out your financial future and stay on course. With defined objectives, you'll be better able to decide how to spend your time, money, and energy.

Improves Dedication and Motivation

When you have a plan for your money, you're more likely to stick to it. Having a specific target in mind increases the likelihood that you will work toward it. Setting and working toward goals gives you direction and motivates you to succeed. Goals are important because they give you something to work for and give you a sense of pride when you reach them.

Enables Accomplishment Evaluation

Achieving monetary success can be gauged through the establishment of certain goals. Reaching your goals allows you to realize how far you've come. Measuring success and failure along the road can help you make necessary adjustments and enjoy your progress along the way. Monitoring your development also serves to keep you honest and energized.

A tool for setting financial priorities

The best way to focus your spending and saving is to set financial goals. When you have a firm grasp on where you want to go, you'll be more equipped to decide how to spend your time and money. If you want to save up for a down payment on a house, for instance, you might decide to reduce your discretionary spending. Your progress toward your monetary goals can be guaranteed if you set spending and saving priorities.

Facilitates Relaxation, monetarily

Financial stress can be alleviated by goal setting. You will feel less stressed and more confident about your financial future if you have a solid strategy in place. Setting objectives might help you feel more in charge of your life and less anxious about the future. The future of your finances, and your peace of mind, can be better predicted with a solid strategy.

Promotes Keeping the Whole Picture in Mind

The act of setting financial objectives instills a mindset of foresight. When you make plans for the future, including your finances, you are not simply considering the here and now. By setting objectives, you can consider your financial legacy and plan for the future. A better understanding of what lies ahead can help you make better choices today that will pay you in the long run.

Ultimately, the key to monetary success is goal planning. The ability to track one's progress toward a goal boosts motivation and dedication, while also facilitating the prioritization of expenditures and savings, easing financial strain, and encouraging long-term planning. You may make substantial progress toward your financial objectives and live the life you want by creating clear goals for yourself and taking action to attain them.

Learn the Secrets of Financial Success by Establishing SMART Objectives

The financial goals you set using the SMART method will be specific, attainable, and quantifiable. Goals should be SMART if they are to be effective. This means that they should be well-defined, quantifiable, timely, and relevant. Here we'll discuss the SMART goal-setting framework and how it can help you achieve your financial dreams.

Specific

A SMART goal is defined by its "specificity," the first component. As a result, you need to have a crystal-clear objective. It's better to make a specific goal like "save $10,000 in a savings account by the end of the year" than to just resolve to "save more money." The steps you need to take to reach your objective become clearer when you use precise language.

Measurable

Second, the objective must be able to be measured. This means that your aim should be quantitative and measurable. If you want to get out of debt, you could tell yourself, "I will pay off $5,000 in credit card debt in the next six months." Having a specific objective makes it easier to gauge your success.

Achievable

Achievability is the third part of the SMART goal framework. Thus, you need to ensure that your objective is both reasonable and doable. It's good to shoot for the stars, but it's not wise to set your sights too high because that can lead to feeling let down. Aiming for $1 million in the following year may be unrealistic if, say, you're now bringing in $50,000 annually. Alternatively, choose an objective that will test your mettle but is still within reach.

Relevant

To round out the acronym, "SMART," relevancy is the fourth component of a successful aim. That's why it's important to make sure your result is in line with the rest of your financial blueprint. A down payment savings goal would be an example of a goal that is both short-term and long-term relevant if the ultimate goal is to purchase a home.

Time-bound

Time constraints are the final element of the SMART goal framework. This indicates that you should establish a time limit for achieving your objective. A year from now would be a good deadline if you want to save $10,000 in a savings account. Having a deadline helps keep you focused and guarantees that you'll reach your objective.

Setting SMART objectives for financial success entails the following steps:

Set some ambitious but achievable financial objectives. I'm curious as to your long-term goals; where do you see yourself in 5, 10, or 20 years?

To achieve your long-term objectives, you need first to divide them into more manageable chunks. The question is, what do you need to do to get to where you want to be in the future?

Make your objectives SMART (specific, measurable, attainable, relevant, and time-bound) by applying this framework.

Put your aspirations on paper and read them frequently. Put your objectives where you will see them frequently.

Make a plan of action to get you closer to your objectives. Just what must you do to get where you want to go?

Keep tabs on how far along you are on the path to success. Make use of a spreadsheet or other methods to monitor your development and make necessary course corrections.

To sum up, the SMART method is useful for making sure that your monetary objectives are specific, measurable, achievable, and time-bound. You can make substantial headway toward your long-term financial goals by setting them up according to the SMART criteria and developing a strategy to achieve them. If you want to succeed financially, it's important to keep track of your accomplishments and revisit your goals frequently.

Effective Methods for Reaching Your Financial Objectives

Much like any other goal, financial ones need more than just a determination to be accomplished. You need a strategy and action to turn your dreams into reality. Some methods for reaching your monetary objectives will be discussed below.

Make a Spending Plan

Making a budget is a vital first step toward reaching your financial objectives.

Creating a budget will help you analyze your income and expenses and find places to make cuts. You can make sure you're making progress toward your financial objectives and effectively use your money by developing a budget.

Put Your Own Money Apart

Before you pay your bills and other costs, you should allot a portion of your income to achieve your financial goals. This can help you stay on track with your financial plans and prioritize what's most important to you. Putting money aside for retirement or other long-term goals can be a challenge, but setting up an automated transfer from your checking account to a savings account or investment account can make it much simpler.

Cut Down on Your Financial Obligations

One of the first steps in getting ahead financially is paying off any outstanding debt. Debts with high-interest rates, such as those incurred by credit cards, can eat away at your disposable income, making it difficult to save or invest. As a first step, focus on eliminating your high-interest debt and then tackle the rest. To make paying off your debts more manageable, you may want to consider taking out a low-interest personal loan to consolidate your existing debts.

How to Raise Your Income

Earning more money can speed up your progress toward your financial objectives. Think about getting a second job, creating a side business, or lobbying for a pay hike. You can also try to find ways to make passive income, like investing in dividend-paying stocks or renting out a room on Airbnb.

Invest in yourself.

You can get far in life by putting money into yourself. Consider boosting your income potential by enrolling in classes or getting credentials. Eating well and exercising frequently are investments that pay off in the form of better health, which in turn can save medical costs and boost productivity.

Try Consulting an Expert

If you need help getting your finances in order, consult an expert. Working with a financial advisor can get you closer to your financial goals because they can help you develop a strategy that is specifically designed for you and your situation. Investment, retirement, and tax counseling are all areas in which they excel.

Maintain Your Drive

Keeping yourself inspired is crucial if you want to reach your financial objectives. Focus on the final objective while also appreciating the tiny victories along the route. Envision yourself succeeding and remind yourself why your objectives are so crucial. One more way to keep yourself motivated and on track is to find an accountability partner, such as a friend or family member.

Be Adaptable

While preparation is essential, so is the ability to adapt. The reality of life is that sometimes you have to pay for things that you didn't plan for. It's important to be flexible with your strategy and open to new opportunities that may hasten your progress.

In conclusion, if you want to succeed financially, you need a strategy, some initiative, and a strong will to succeed. You may make substantial progress toward your financial goals by making a budget, paying yourself first, paying down debt, growing your income, investing in yourself, seeking professional guidance, keeping motivated, and being flexible. Focus on the process, rather than the result, as you work toward your financial goals.

Chapter 4

How to Conquer Your Fears and Self-Limiting Beliefs

The obstacles that prevent people from reaching their financial goals are discussed in this chapter, with a particular emphasis on overcoming limiting ideas and fear. It delves into the most widespread money-related misconceptions and anxieties and offers solutions for getting past them.

* Methods for Recognizing Self-Limiting Attitudes and Prejudices
* Dismantling and Reconstructing Your Self-Limiting Attitudes and Ideas
* Techniques for Conquering Financial Anxiety and Self-Doubt

How to Recognize Self-Limiting Thoughts and Feelings

The first step toward overcoming the obstacles keeping you from reaching your financial goals is becoming aware of the negative thoughts and feelings holding you back. Self-limiting ideas can hamper a person's ability to reach their full potential. They usually develop due to prior experience, criticism, or socialization. Concerns are feelings brought on by apprehension of some kind of risk. It doesn't matter if they're genuine or imagined; both types can hinder your progress.

It would be best if you first looked within yourself, at your ideas and feelings, to discover what it is that is holding you back. Ask yourself, "What do I believe about money and financial success?" "What are my biggest anxieties related to money?" and "What negative self-talk do I participate in regarding success?" can help. Consider how your personal history may have shaped your current set of self-defeating assumptions and concerns.

Record your negative thoughts and feelings once you've pinpointed them. You'll have a better understanding of them and be more equipped to combat them if you do this. Realize that your preconceived notions and irrational concerns are merely the product of your unique perspective and a history of experiences.

Beliefs like "money is evil," "money is hard to come by," and "rich people are greedy" are all frequent limiting beliefs when it comes to financial success. The pessimistic outlook and narrowed perspective that result from holding such views can prohibit you from taking the steps necessary to achieve financial success. Financial anxiety can stem from apprehensions about succeeding, failing, taking risks, or losing money.

It takes considerable introspection and self-reflection to recognize your own limiting ideas and fears. The first step toward overcoming these obstacles and realizing financial success is to recognize and accept these thoughts and feelings for what they are.

Dismantling and Reconstructing Your Self-Limiting Attitudes and Ideas

Having recognized your self-defeating ideas and phobias, you can then begin to question and reframe them. Reframing is creating new, empowering ideas that will support your financial success after you've challenged your limiting beliefs and anxieties.

Asking yourself questions like "Is this belief/fear true?", "What evidence do I have to support this belief/fear?" and "What would happen if I didn't believe/fear this anymore?" can help you examine limiting beliefs and fears. The answers to these questions will help you start to recognize that your ideas and concerns are frequently not founded in fact but in your vision and your personal history.

Positive affirmations are an excellent tool for rethinking and redefining limiting ideas and anxieties. Affirmations are phrases of encouragement that one repeats to oneself frequently to solidify the adoption of a more favorable worldview. Affirmations like "I attract prosperity and abundance into my life" or "Money is a tool for me to achieve my objectives and help others" might help you reframe a limiting thought like "money is evil" to a more positive one.

Visualization as though you have already reached your financial goals is another method for re-framing your limiting beliefs and concerns. Having a clear mental picture of your accomplishments might help you develop an optimistic outlook and push over self-defeating assumptions and inhibitions. If you want to be a millionaire, for instance, you could see yourself with a mansion, a sports vehicle, and plenty of leisure time.

It's crucial to keep in mind that it takes time and effort to challenge and reframe your limiting ideas and anxieties. It's unrealistic to expect to break free of all of your self-limiting ideas and anxieties in a single leap of faith. Yet, with regular application of these methods, you may retrain your brain to adopt more helpful patterns of thought that will ultimately contribute to your financial success.

Avoiding or repressing one's limiting ideas and anxieties is a common blunder that people make when trying to overcome them. Nevertheless, in the long run, this strategy fails because your fears and beliefs will continue to hold you back until you actively work to overcome them. Instead, you should confront your limiting assumptions and concerns head-on and work towards your goals.

It also helps to have supportive group of friends and family who will inspire and motivate you to succeed in reaching your financial objectives. It's important to avoid the company of negative people who constantly criticize or minimize your ambitions, as they will only serve to reinforce your limiting beliefs and concerns.

In conclusion, if you want to succeed financially, you need to challenge and reframe your limiting beliefs and anxieties. The key to changing your thinking and realizing your full potential is to become aware of the negative thoughts and feelings that are holding you back, evaluate their veracity, and replace them with more positive ones. Investing in yourself in this way can lead to financial and personal improvement, but it can also take time and work.

Restricting Thoughts and Afraid of Financial Success: Techniques

If you want to be financially successful, you must conquer your doubts and fears. The following are some methods that have helped others face their money worries and aspirations head-on:

Understanding one's own limiting assumptions and concerns is the first step in overcoming them. Be mindful of what comes up in your mind about wealth and success in your financial endeavors. Document your thoughts and evaluate them later. Consider whether your beliefs are founded in reality or simply your own biases.

You can overcome self-limiting beliefs by recasting them in a more empowering light. By shifting one's point of view, one might "reframe" a problem or issue. Instead of telling yourself things like "I can't be successful because I'm not good enough," try telling yourself things like "I am good enough, and I have what it takes to be successful." It may be helpful to reframe your beliefs to get a new perspective and resolve to act.

As a means of reinforcing your newfound good ideas and behaviors, try using affirmations. Affirmations like "I am worthy of financial abundance" or "Money flows readily and naturally into my life" might help you reframe limiting beliefs like "I'll never be rich." Use these affirmations as a daily ritual to instill in yourself a new set of empowering thoughts and attitudes.

Imagine yourself already successful, and you'll be well on your way to overcoming the obstacles standing in your way. Imagine that you have already attained your monetary objectives. Imagine having the means to buy the house of your dreams, the car of your dreams, and the time and flexibility to do as you choose. Having a clear mental picture of your accomplishments might help you develop an optimistic outlook and push over self-defeating assumptions and inhibitions.

Taking action is the single most crucial step toward overcoming self-limiting thoughts and worries. Take baby steps if you're nervous about trying new things. To achieve your financial goals, start slow and progressively expand your risk exposure. The key to overcoming your fear of failure is to recognize that it is an inevitable part of the process and that every setback is an opportunity to grow.

Make an effort to find a group of positive and encouraging people who can help you stay motivated and on track to realize your financial objectives. It's important to avoid the company of negative people who constantly criticize or minimize your ambitions, as they will only serve to reinforce your limiting beliefs and concerns. Find a mentor or coach who can guide you through the process of overcoming self-limiting thoughts and behaviors so that you can reach your financial objectives.

If you've accomplished something, no matter how small, you should be proud of yourself. Gaining the drive to keep going and reinforcing your new, empowered thoughts and attitudes by celebrating your victories is a win-win. Acknowledge and reward yourself for each achievement along the way to show yourself that you can succeed in reaching your financial objectives.

To sum up, if you want to be financially successful, you must conquer your limiting beliefs and your fear of failure. You may overcome your limiting beliefs and anxieties and reach your financial objectives by self-awareness practice, reframing your beliefs, utilizing positive affirmations, visualizing achievement, taking action, seeking help, and celebrating successes. The rewards of material success and personal development are well worth the time and effort it takes to overcome limiting beliefs and concerns.

Chapter 5

Creating Forward Progress

This chapter will teach you how to make progress toward your financial goals regularly, and how to sustain that progress over time. The book discusses the value of adopting a growth mentality and provides actionable advice for gaining financial footing.

- ★ How to Make a Strategy That Will Guarantee Your Financial Success
- ★ Successful financial behavior modification
- ★ Gaining Steam for Financial Success

How to Make a Strategy That Will Guarantee Your Financial Success

Establishing a course of action is essential for reaching one's financial goals. When you don't have a plan, it's tough to know what to do, when, and how to get it done. An action plan empowers people to take charge of their economic futures by articulating the measures that must be taken.

Developing a successful financial strategy entails the following steps

Write Out Your Objectives

Establishing what you hope to achieve monetarily is the first stage in formulating a strategy to achieve those goals. Create a list of both immediate and far-off goals to get started. Paying off credit card debt in a year, buying a house in five, or reaching a certain income level in ten years are all time-bound examples of such goals. Having clear objectives will help you focus your efforts and achieve success.

If you want to achieve your goals, you need to break them down into manageable chunks.

Now that you know what you want to do, you can start breaking it down into manageable chunks. Having this information will facilitate the development of a workable and realistic strategy. Suppose you want to pay off your credit card debt in one year. In that case, you can do so by dividing the overall task into more manageable chunks like setting a budget, cutting back on expenses, earning more money, and making regular payments.

Identify the Timeframe

Your next step after breaking down your objectives into manageable chunks should be choosing a deadline. Establishing due dates for individual tasks is a crucial part of this process. Take into account your existing financial condition, your other obligations, and your circumstances while establishing a deadline.

Find Out What You'll Need

You may need to invest in your education, training, equipment, or capital to reach your financial objectives. Find out what you'll need to accomplish each mission and how you'll get it. Saving for a down payment, getting assistance from a financial advisor, and taking classes on money management are all good examples of this.

Keep tabs on your development

Having a plan of action in place is not sufficient for monetary success. To make sure you are on track, you should check in on your development frequently. Adjust your strategy as needed by reviewing it frequently. As a result, you'll be more likely to maintain your drive and dedication.

You Should Be Proud of Your Successes

Last but not least, remember to reward yourself for your progress along the journey. If you want to keep moving forward, you need to recognize and praise yourself after every success. Gaining a sense of fulfillment from commemorating your successes can encourage you to keep working toward your financial objectives.

To sum up, the first step toward achieving your financial goals is to develop a strategy for doing so. The steps are:

- Deciding what you want to accomplish.

- Breaking it down into manageable chunks.
- Setting a plan.
- Figuring out how long it will take and what resources you'll need.
- Keeping tabs on your progress.
- Rewarding yourself when you finish.

If you stick to these guidelines, you should soon be enjoying the fruits of your labor financially.

Successful financial behavior modification

Making a plan and sticking to it is crucial to your financial success. Achieving your goals requires consistent, positive behavior. There is great power in the little things we do repeatedly throughout time. In this chapter, we'll discuss some of the most important routines followed by wealthy people and how you might begin to adopt these practices for yourself.

Budgeting

Creating and sticking to a budget is a crucial skill for ensuring your financial security. To do this, you need to make a monthly spending plan that takes into account both your income and your outgoings. Making a budget is a great way to keep from spending more than you earn monthly. You can also look for places where you can save money, like eating out or going to the movies, and put that money toward savings or paying off debt.

If you want to make a budget that works, you need first to keep track of your spending for a month or two. The next step is to determine how you will spend your money monthly and record that information in a spreadsheet or a budgeting tool. Expenses like rent or mortgage, utilities, food, transportation, and debt payments should all be factored in. Your budget should also include room for investments and other forms of savings and discretionary spending like entertainment and travel.

Saving

The practice of saving money is another crucial behavior for monetary success. Saving is reserving a specific amount of money each month for use in the future, whether for retirement, unexpected expenses, or a down payment on a home. Consistent savings over time can assist achieve financial security and independence.

Establish a monthly savings target that takes into account your budget and long-term financial objectives. If you want to save money without thinking about it, set up a monthly direct deposit or automated transfer from your checking account to a savings account. Doing so will allow your funds to increase without any effort on your part.

Investing

For sustainable wealth over time, investing is a must. You can invest in the stock market, real estate, or other assets to increase your wealth over time. While risk is always involved with investing, the potential reward might be far greater than that of a traditional savings account.

Before making your first commitment, learning about the many investment options and settling on a plan that fits your objectives and comfort level is essential. Among many other things, you can put your money into stocks, mutual funds, ETFs, and even real estate. A financial advisor can assist you in creating an investment plan tailored to your specific needs.

Debt Avoidance

Avoiding debt is another crucial behavior for a healthy financial future. While taking on debt to make large purchases like a house or fund a college education might be a great decision in certain circumstances, it can also be a big cause of worry and financial hardship if not handled properly. When you have a lot of debt, you have to put a lot of your monthly money toward paying it off, making it harder to save for the future or pay off other important expenses.

Keep your expenses low and your income steady to avoid debt. You can also make an effort to settle any outstanding debt, such as credit card bills or student loans, as soon as you can. Making sacrifices like reducing frivolous spending or taking on additional work to raise income may be necessary.

Constant Education

In conclusion, long-term financial success necessitates the formation of a habit of continual learning. Because of this, it's crucial for financial professionals to constantly learn new information and adapt to new market conditions.

Gaining Steam for Financial Success

It takes more than simply goal-setting and a plan of action to succeed monetarily. Building momentum and maintaining motivation to keep working toward those targets are also essential.

Building momentum toward monetary targets is the focus of this chapter.

Recognize even the smallest victories

Gaining momentum is facilitated by recognizing and rewarding even the smallest of accomplishments. Accomplishing even a relatively modest accomplishment can significantly boost morale and assurance. Rewarding yourself for your efforts helps keep you motivated and optimistic while you work toward your goals. If you want to save $10,000, you can reward yourself with $1,000, $2,000, and so on along the way.

Put yourself in a position to succeed by surrounding yourself with good people.

The individuals that support and encourage you go a long way toward determining your level of drive and achievement. Assuring that supportive people surround you will help you maintain your motivation and drive to succeed. Get yourself some successful pals or mentors who have been where you want to go financially. If you need extra help staying motivated and accountable, joining a support group or online community may be the answer.

Don't stop educating yourself.

Maintaining your drive and making progress toward your objectives can be aided by continuing your education in the realms of personal finance and investment. Knowing more about personal finance can increase self-assurance and independence. If you want to learn more, you can do so by reading books, going to seminars and workshops, or enrolling in online courses.

Engage in some form of self-care.

If you want to gain momentum and succeed financially, you need to take care of yourself physically and emotionally. Making time for self-care activities like exercise, meditation, or spending time with loved ones is essential because stress and burnout can undermine your efforts. You'll have greater stamina and mental clarity to work for your financial objectives if you take care of yourself first.

Monitor your development

Keeping tabs on your development can help you gain momentum and maintain your drive. It's a visual reminder of how far you've gone and an encouragement to keep going. Use a spreadsheet or a mobile app to maintain tabs on your cash flow, investments, and savings. Schedule time to check in with yourself at regular intervals so that you can assess your progress and make necessary adjustments to your strategy.

Segregate your objectives into manageable steps.

If you want to reach your financial goals, it may help to break them down into smaller, more doable activities. If you want to get out of debt, for instance, you can divide the process into smaller steps like preparing a budget, talking to your creditors, and paying more on the principal. Getting through each baby step can boost your confidence and encourage you to keep going.

Plan for success by visualizing it.

Seeing yourself succeed financially is a great incentive. Think about how your life will change once you've accomplished your objectives. Think about what it would be like to be financially independent and all the doors that would open to you. Making a vision board or engaging in guided meditation are two methods for visualizing success and keeping one's eye on the prize.

Take note that if you want to build momentum toward financial success, you need to employ a variety of techniques, including rewarding yourself for small victories, surrounding yourself with supportive people, never stop learning, prioritizing your well-being, keeping detailed records of your activities, dividing your goals into manageable chunks, and visualizing your accomplishment. You can create the momentum you need to reach your financial objectives and live the life of your dreams by following these steps and keeping yourself inspired.

Chapter 6

Establishing Alternative Revenue Sources

The necessity of income diversity and the methods for generating numerous revenue streams are discussed in this chapter. Methods of making extra money, such as passive income streams and investments, are discussed, along with more concrete advice.

- ★ Recognizing the Value of Many Sources of Income
- ★ Developing and Maintaining a Diverse Income Stream Strategy Set

Realizing the Value of Having a Stable Income From Many Sources

With the state of the economy as it is, relying on a single salary is no longer a safe bet for your family's financial future. It is now widely recognized that relying on a single source of income is unsafe due to the volatility of the employment market, the rapid evolution of many industries, and the cyclical nature of the economy. Having a variety of income sources can make you feel more secure, lessen your exposure to financial risk, and open up new avenues for professional and personal development.

If you have various ways to make money at once, you are said to have multiple income streams. These multiple income streams may be a full-time or part-time job, rental or investment income, a second career, or freelancing. Diversification is the key to a prosperous financial future. Having a variety of income sources is crucial for those who want to amass riches.

First, your earning potential rises when you have more than one source of income. There is a cap on how much money you can make if you rely on a single job or another source of revenue. Having multiple sources of revenue allows you to supplement your main source of income and even increase your earnings.

Second, having a variety of income sources helps cushion the blow of a layoff or a dip in the economy. If you have multiple income streams rather than just one, you can weather the loss of one without becoming broke. Having a safety net of many sources of income can make you feel more secure about your financial situation.

Third, having a variety of income sources allows you more leeway in the direction you take in your financial life. Consider how much more quickly you may reach your financial goals if you have numerous sources of income, such as when saving for retirement. It enables one to pursue one's passions or interests without giving up one's main source of income.

Having a diverse income portfolio is associated with increased financial stability and independence. It allows for expansion, lessens danger, and accelerates attaining monetary objectives.

Next, we'll go through some strategies for locating viable revenue channels.

Looking for Possible Sources of Funding

The key to financial independence is to diversify one's income. When you have multiple ways to bring in money, you spread your earnings and reduce your vulnerability. In this chapter, we'll discuss the best ways to find new revenue streams that align with your unique interests, abilities, and available resources.

Think About Your Abilities

Assessing your abilities is the first step in locating new sources of revenue. Try reflecting on your strengths and interests. Evaluate your past employment, academic background, extracurricular activities, and interests. Think about how you can use your skills to benefit those around you.

Writers, for instance, might advertise their skills to corporate clients and private clients as freelancers. If you have a knack for visual communication, you can use it to make a living by creating logos, brochures, and websites for businesses. Offering online classes or consulting services is a great way to capitalize on your knowledge and experience.

Discover Alternative Commercial Structures

After you've figured out your unique set of strengths, you can start looking into company opportunities that put those strengths to use. **Among the numerous** viable business paradigms are the following:

1. Giving clients your undivided attention on a project-by-project basis is a definition of freelancing.
2. Consulting is the practice of advising clients as subject-matter experts.
3. Online retail through Amazon, Etsy, and Shopify; is known as electronic commerce.
4. Affiliate marketing promotes other people's items in exchange for a percentage of those sales.
5. Profitable real estate investment can come from either long-term renting or quick house flipping.

6. Investing is putting money into stocks, bonds, or other assets that produce residual income.

Every possible business structure has benefits and drawbacks; you should pick the one that best fits your personality, values, and aspirations.

Consider the Competition and Market Needs

Market demand and competitiveness are also crucial factors to consider when trying to find new sources of revenue. It would be best to guarantee that people will pay for your expertise and that you can set yourself apart from the competitors.

You can gauge the level of interest in a product or service by conducting market research to learn more about a potential customer base's wants, needs, and buying habits. Google Trends, Amazon's Best Sellers, and social media analytics are some of the tools you can use to learn about your niche's most popular topics of conversation.

You may assess the level of competition by looking at your competitors' pricing plans, marketing approaches, and strengths and shortcomings. You could also fill a void in the market that your rivals have ignored.

Put Your Hypotheses to the Test

Once you have found possible income streams, you should test and confirm your ideas before wasting time or resources. In other words, you need to ensure that your ideas can be implemented, will produce money, and can be scaled up.

Developing a minimum viable product (MVP) and releasing it to the public is a good technique to gauge interest in your ideas. If you want to start selling an online course, for instance, all you need is a landing page that briefly describes the content, and a means to pre-order it. Once there is enough demand for your course, you can begin developing and providing its materials.

In addition to consulting experts, conducting a pilot study and analyzing the data can help you confirm the validity of your hypotheses. To launch a podcast, you could record a few episodes and then monitor their reception via metrics like downloads, reviews, and shares on social media. A successful podcast can lead to growth and additional episode production, which can lead to the sale of swag, commercials, and sponsorships.

To sum up, you need to do some introspection, study the marketplace, and experiment to determine where your money could go. You can generate multiple sources of income by capitalizing on your abilities, investigating potential business models, researching the needs of your target market, and putting your ideas to the test.

Methods for Establishing and Supervising Various Sources of Income

Achieving financial independence and amassing riches can be accomplished through the development of several sources of income. The goal is to have several streams of money coming in at once, both as a safety net and a means to reach your end goals more quickly. In this chapter, we'll discuss methods for developing and coordinating separate sources of revenue.

Explore your interests and abilities.

Finding your strengths and interests is an important first step in developing several income streams. To do this, you must first identify your strengths and passions. Finding new ways to make money is possible when you use your talents and interests to start a business or provide a service.

If you enjoy writing, you could shop as a freelance writer or publish your books. If you're musically gifted, you should form a band or offer lessons to others. By capitalizing on your strengths and interests, you can set up a variety of enjoyable and fulfilling revenue streams.

Create multiple avenues of revenue.

Diversifying your income by developing several sources is a smart strategy. This strategy necessitates having many redundant methods of financial support. You have multiple revenue streams to fall back on if one of them fails or experiences a downturn.

One such mix could include rental homes, stock investments, and a side company. The income from your stock assets and your side business can assist in offsetting any losses you incur should the rental market decline. Having multiple sources of income helps spread out your risk and provides a safety net in case of financial trouble.

Consider putting money into sources of passive income.

With little ongoing effort, you can build many income streams using passive income. Earnings that need little to no effort on your part are called passive income. Rental income, stock dividends, and intellectual property royalties are all examples of passive income.

Putting your money into passive income streams can give you a steady stream of money with minimal maintenance. A good example of a passive source of income is dividend-paying stocks, which may be purchased and held for years without any further effort on your part. Similar to how owning rental properties can give a steady income stream if managed well.

Launch a part-time endeavor

One viable option for generating additional revenue is to launch a side business. A side hustle can range from being a part-time activity to a full-time occupation. The trick is to foresee a gap in the market and build a company to fill it.

Although it takes time and money to get a side business up and running, it's worth it if you want to pursue your interests while making money. Starting a business is exciting, but it takes careful preparation to ensure long-term success.

It would be best if you learned to time-manage

Having a full-time job or other obligations can make it difficult to create additional income streams. The ability to keep and expand your sources of income depends on your ability to manage your time wisely.

Focusing on the most important sources of revenue is one method to manage your time better. Determine which of your revenue streams brings in the most money, and put your efforts there. Doing so will ensure you make the most of your time and money.

Automating or delegating chores is another method of time management. If, for instance, you own rental properties, you may have a management firm deal with the day-to-day operations on your behalf. Your time will then be freed up, allowing you to concentrate on expanding alternative means of financial gain.

In conclusion, attaining financial independence and amassing riches can be accomplished through the development of several sources of income. You can create multiple sources of income that serve as a safety net and help you reach your financial goals if you put in the time and effort required to assess your skills and interests, diversify your income streams, invest in passive income streams, launch a side business, and effectively manage your time.

Chapter 7

Investing for Financial Success

In this chapter, you'll learn the basics of investing and get an overview of the many financial vehicles at your disposal. Long-term wealth creation is discussed, as is the significance of understanding risk and return, developing a diverse portfolio, and other practical investment recommendations.

- ★ A Foundational Knowledge of Investing for Financial Success
- ★ How to Identify Wealth-Building Investment Opportunities and Use Them to Your Advantage

How to Grow Your Money Via Investing

Investment is crucial to accumulating wealth and establishing financial independence. Nonetheless, many individuals, especially newcomers, find it to be a frightening and unsettling subject.

If you want to learn more about investing and how to increase your wealth, this chapter will lay the groundwork for you.

To begin, you must have a firm grasp of the concept of investing. Investing is, at its heart, the process of putting money to work to earn one's risk tolerance and time horizon, this may entail investing in stocks, bonds, mutual funds, real estate, or some combination of these. Investments are made so that, in the long run, the investor will have more wealth than they did initially.

Considering the potential benefits against the potential losses is a crucial part of every investment strategy. Typically, the higher the possible return of an investment, the higher the associated risk. Investments in stocks, for instance, might yield substantial profits, but they also have a higher risk of loss than, say, bonds or real estate. When determining where to place your money, knowing your risk tolerance and the dangers associated with various investing options is crucial.

Diversification is another crucial thing to think about. Spreading your money out among several different assets is called "diversification," and it's done so to lower overall investment risk. Put all your money into one stock, and you place all your eggs in one basket. The capital loss could be substantial if the stock fails to meet expectations. If you invest in various stocks and other assets like bonds and real estate, you can reduce the impact of any single market decline.

A wide range of investment opportunities exists, each with its own set of pros and cons. **Most investors put their money into one of these popular types of investments:**

A stock is a certificate of ownership in a corporation. But, when you purchase stock in a company, you become the proud owner of a fraction of the business. You can make money off of your investment in the company if its stock price rises. Your investment may be at risk if the firm underperforms and the value of your shares drops.

Investment bonds are issued by a government or a corporation and allow investors to lend money to these entities for a specified period with the promise of interest payments. Although bonds carry less risk than stocks, their returns are often lower.

Investing in real estate is acquiring and overseeing assets to maximize profit, either through rental or eventual resale. Although rewarding, investment in real estate calls for substantial initial funding and continuing administration.

Mutual Funds: A mutual fund is a pooled investment vehicle that uses the combined capital of many people to buy a diversified basket of securities, including stocks, bonds, and other financial instruments. Those who desire to diversify their holdings but lack the knowledge or time to do so on their own may find this a suitable choice.

No matter what kind of investment you decide to make, you should always do your homework and be aware of the possible outcomes. You can do this by getting the advice of a financial expert, reading up on the topic on your own, or even enrolling in some online classes.

It's not enough to know the ropes when it comes to investing; you also need a solid plan. You can do this by deciding what you want to accomplish with your assets (like retirement or a down payment on a house) and developing a strategy to get you there. Long-term investment management involves doing things like monitoring your portfolio regularly and making changes as necessary.

In general, investment is an effective means of amassing wealth and gaining independence from one's financial situation. Readers may achieve their financial goals by learning the fundamentals of investing and creating a solid investment strategy.

The Process of Finding Investing Opportunities to Create Wealth

To amass riches and secure one's financial future, investing is essential. There are many investment opportunities, but it might be difficult to narrow down your choices to just one. Use these guidelines to zero in on the investments that can help you reach your financial objectives.

Set some concrete, monetary objectives.

Having a clear idea of where you want your money to go is the first step in finding the right investment options. Exactly why are you putting money aside? Is it for your future retirement, the higher education of your children, a down payment on a home, or something else entirely? Achievable investments can be found if you have a firm grasp on what it is you hope to accomplish with your savings.

Investing in a 401(k) or an individual retirement account (IRA) could be a good choice if you're planning for your retirement (IRA). A high-yield savings account or a certificate of deposit could be good options for those saving for a home's down payment (CD). If you know what you want to do with your money, you can better narrow down your investing choices.

Think about what you're willing to risk.

Consider your level of comfort with risk as another criterion for selecting investments. Do you feel safe taking on high-risk investments with the potential for huge returns, or do you prefer to play it safe with low-risk investments that provide smaller returns?

Investments in stocks and mutual funds carry a higher level of risk than those in bonds or certificates of deposit. Higher gains are possible, but so is the possibility of greater losses.

Before making any financial commitments, you should determine how much risk you will take. If you're a novice investor or prefer to play it safe, you should begin with lower-risk investments and work your way up to more daring bets as you gain experience.

It would be best if you thought about how long you have to invest.

The time frame in which you can make these investments is also important. For what period do you anticipate keeping your current portfolio? How long do you plan on keeping your investments?

Liquid investments, like equities and mutual funds, are good options for short-term investors. These investments are great for short-term portfolios because they can be acquired and traded easily.

Investments with a longer time horizon, like real estate or a 401(k), are more suitable for long-term savers and investors (k). The potential for higher returns over time means waiting longer for these assets to mature.

Learn the facts.

It would be best if you started looking into investment options once you have a firm grasp on your desired result, level of risk, and time horizon for making a financial commitment. Online, you can find a wealth of information, such as specialized investment blogs, financial news websites, and discussion forums.

If you want to invest money, you must do your homework first. Choose investments with a history of success that fit with your financial objectives and level of risk tolerance.

Seeking the help of a financial counselor is another option worth considering. A financial advisor is there to help you through the maze of investment options and give you advice that is tailored to your specific needs.

In conclusion, it is important to consider your financial goals, risk tolerance, investing schedule, and research while trying to locate investment opportunities. Investing wisely that serves your needs and goals can be accomplished through careful goal setting and a realistic risk tolerance assessment.

Methods for Making Smart Investments and Reaching Your Financial Goals

Achieving financial independence requires prudent investment. Whether you're a first-time investor or have been in the game for a while, it's important to have a plan that fits your objectives and comfort level with risk. Investing correctly is one of the best ways to grow your money and secure your financial future, and we'll talk about some of those options in this chapter.

Think About Your Investing Objectives and Risk Appetite

Evaluating your investment objectives and comfort level with risk before making any purchases is important. Investing with a certain end in mind is important, whether that end is far off or just around the corner. How well you can handle market volatility and the possibility of financial loss is a measure of your risk tolerance.

The success of your investment strategy depends on your ability to set reasonable expectations and know how much risk you are willing to take. Investments like bonds and mutual funds are good choices for those who want to minimize their chance of loss. You can put your money into stocks or other high-risk assets if you have a high-risk tolerance.

Invest in a Variety of Assets

One of the most important ways to invest properly is through diversification. Diversifying your holdings among equities, bonds, and real estate is crucial. In this manner, the underperformance of a single asset class will have a smaller effect on your portfolio as a whole.

It is also wise to diversify your holdings within each asset type. If you want to diversify your risk, you can invest in several sectors and companies on the stock market, for instance. Diversifying your holdings effectively reduces your exposure to market fluctuations and boosts your prospects of long-term success.

A long-term investment is a way to go.

A second crucial tactic for amassing wealth through investing is to do it over extended periods. The best investors think long-term and resist the temptation to time the market or pursue rapid rewards.

Long-term investing entails keeping your eye on the prize rather than selling your holdings for a while. With the power of compound interest, you can enhance your earnings with this tactic. Short-term market volatility, which can be unanticipated and lead to poor investing decisions, is also mitigated.

Think About Your Financial Choices

There is a wide variety of investment opportunities available. Stocks, bonds, mutual funds, exchange-traded funds (ETFs), real estate, and alternative investments like private equity are some of the most popular choices for investors.

One must thoroughly weigh each investment opportunity's benefits and drawbacks before making a choice. For instance, stocks have the potential for high returns but also carry a high risk. But bonds are a safer investment alternative, albeit one with lower returns.

Whereas real estate investments can increase one's net worth greatly, they also necessitate a large initial outlay of cash and can be more difficult to oversee than other types of investments. Private equity and other forms of alternative investing can offer diversification and higher returns than more traditional investment vehicles. Still, they often demand a larger initial commitment and are less liquid.

Maintain Awareness and Evaluate Your Approach

Lastly, if you want to succeed in the long run with your investments, you need to keep yourself well-informed and review your approach frequently. The market is volatile. Therefore, it's important to be abreast of the latest developments.

Your investing plan should be reviewed regularly to ensure it continues to align with your objectives and comfort level with risk. You may need to change your plan as you move closer to retirement or accomplish other life goals.

In conclusion, making prudent investments is crucial to accumulating money and obtaining financial independence. You can improve your chances of long-term success in the stock market by setting investment goals and establishing your comfort level with risk, diversifying your portfolio, investing for the long term, thinking about your investment options, and keeping up to date with market news and trends, as well as by regularly reevaluating your strategy.

Chapter 8

Cultivating a Sense of abundance

Discover the secrets of cultivating an attitude of plenty and bringing more money into your life in this chapter. It delves into the value of thankfulness, charity, and benevolence and offers methods for cultivating an attitude of plenty.

★ Gaining an understanding of the abundance mentality
★ How to Go Beyond a Lack-Based Worldview
★ Practicing appreciation for one's blessings.

Gaining an understanding of the abundance mentality

The term "abundance mindset" describes a way of thinking in which one prioritizes opportunities and possibilities over perceived constraints. It's a way of thinking that influences one's outlook on life and the world around them. Those with an "abundance mindset" are confident in their abilities and the potential for success in the world, and they believe they can accomplish anything they set their minds to.

Achieving financial success requires adopting this mindset since it fosters an optimistic view of wealth and income. The former allows for more opportunities to grow financially secure, whereas the latter emphasizes deficits and lack. People with an abundance attitude don't let their current circumstances hold them back but rather use them as a springboard for further development.

The importance of abundance in all aspects of life, not just material possessions, is emphasized by those with an abundant mindset. Well-being incorporates physical well-being, social well-being, intellectual advancement, and spiritual evolution. The idea of abundance is more than just having plenty of stuff; it extends to all aspects of one's existence.

Those who have adopted an abundance mindset know that their present circumstances do not constrain their potential for development and achievement. Instead of seeing problems as impediments, they see them as learning experiences. They are not hesitant to try new things because they understand that making mistakes is a necessary part of the learning process.

The assurance that there is enough for everyone is also crucial to adopt an abundance mentality. The idea that there isn't enough to go around and that people must fight for what they want is foreign to those who adopt an abundance attitude. They have a more optimistic view of the world, where plenty of possibilities exist for those who work hard and contribute to society.

In a nutshell, having an abundant mindset means constantly looking for ways to improve yourself and your situation. Believing that there is enough for everyone necessitates a mindset shift from one of scarcity to one of abundance. Those who take on an attitude of abundance are better able to help themselves and others, as well as the world at large, prosper.

How to Go Beyond a Lack-Based Worldview

Having a "scarcity mentality" is a negative perspective regarding resources, opportunity, or riches. This worldview holds that there is no such thing as a free lunch; that everyone's success is someone else's failure. People who believe in scarcity are more likely to be plagued by negative emotions such as worry, anxiety, and distrust, all of which might impede their progress toward material prosperity.

Conquering a sense of scarcity is a crucial first step in embracing a more productive way of thinking. To do so, one must become aware of and combat limiting ideas that foster a scarcity mindset, such as "I can't afford it," "I'll never be able to save enough," and "There isn't enough money to go around." It is possible to begin a journey toward a more productive way of thinking by recasting these ideas in more positive terms and replacing them with positive affirmations.

Focusing on appreciation is a potent tool for overcoming a scarcity mindset. It can be helpful to alter one's attitude from scarcity to abundance by practicing thankfulness for what one already possesses. Keeping a gratitude notebook, meditating, or even just pausing each day briefly to consider one's many blessings are all great ways to cultivate an attitude of thankfulness.

Changing one's perspective from scarcity to growth and plenty is another strategy for overcoming the "not enough" mentality. In other words, rather than focusing on one's lack of money, one should look for ways to increase and diversify their holdings. Individuals might start developing an attitude of prosperity and optimism by emphasizing what is possible.

Last but not least, we must acknowledge fear's function in maintaining a scarcity mindset. Individuals may hesitate to take chances and work for their financial goals out of fear of failure, rejection, or the unknown. Individuals can start to develop the self-assurance and resiliency necessary for financial success by facing their concerns head-on.

In conclusion, if you want to create a life of plenty, you must get over your fear of running out of resources. Individuals can begin to alter their thinking towards abundance and attain more financial success by addressing limiting beliefs, concentrating on gratitude and progress, and overcoming fear.

Practicing thanksgiving for one's blessings

One must change their focus from lack to plenty to develop a culture of plenty. We need to stop complaining and start appreciating the things we do have. An attitude of gratitude serves as the cornerstone of a prosperous outlook, opening our eyes to possibilities for development and achievement that might otherwise go unnoticed.

Focusing on lack causes us to worry and be concerned about the future. Many of us stress about needing more of something, whether it is cash, time, or materials. These unpleasant feelings impair decision-making and make us reluctant to try new things or seize exciting opportunities. But when we change our perspective to one of plenty, we view things in a new light. In our thoughts, the sky is the limit, and if we put in the effort, we can accomplish everything we set our minds to.

Keeping a gratitude notebook is one practice that might help you develop an attitude of thankfulness. To accomplish this, record three things you are thankful for each day. Doing so can help rewire your brain to look for the bright side rather than dwell on the bad. You will gradually become more positive and perceive more prospects for development and achievement.

Gratitude can be developed further by showing appreciation to those around you. Not only does it make us feel better on the inside, but it also helps us bond with those around us. The potential for further cooperation and development is enhanced. An attitude of abundance can be developed by appreciating the good in your life and showing gratitude to those who have helped you along the way.

Maintaining a positive attitude and an abundance mindset does not mean we should ignore difficulties. Nonetheless, it does include taking an optimistic and constructive stance in the face of these difficulties. Finding positive ways of thinking and expanding our horizons is preferable to dwelling on the bad. When we view the world through the lens of abundance, we can see setbacks for what they are: chances to improve ourselves.

Developing an attitude of plenty helps to be kind and caring to oneself. This entails giving equal attention to your physical, mental, and emotional well-being. Taking care of oneself enables one to view difficulties as chances for growth and success.

Gratitude is one way, but there are additional practices that can help you shift into an attitude of plenty. Visualization is one such technique. When you visualize your achievement and the positive emotions that come with it, you are more likely to achieve your goals. When we imagine achieving our goals, we condition our minds to anticipate only the good results we seek.

To achieve success, another tactic is to look for abundance in every facet of life, not only material things. This involves taking stock of the many blessings in your life, such as those of love, joy, and health. A more cheerful mindset can aid in attaining monetary goals when one focuses on abundance across all areas of life.

Last but not least, put oneself in an encouraging and supportive environment. It's important to associate with people who will encourage you and who have a constructive outlook on life. In a supportive environment, we are more likely to have faith in ourselves and to perceive possibilities for development and achievement.

The ability to maintain an attitude of abundance is crucial to your financial well-being, so it's worth your time to work on developing it. If we change our mindset from one of scarcity to one of abundance, we'll be able to see and take advantage of new avenues for development and advancement. Having an abundance mindset may be fostered in several ways, including through the cultivation of gratitude, the practice of self-compassion and self-care, and the cultivation of a positive and supportive environment. One's chances of achieving one's financial goals and leading a happy, abundant life are enhanced when one adopts a growth mindset and an optimistic outlook on life.

Chapter 9

Sustaining Your Drive and Upward Progress

The chapter's main focus is on how to keep going strong over the long haul. Achieving financial independence is discussed, along with the significance of holding oneself accountable, relishing in one's triumphs, and maintaining a broad perspective.

- ★ The Importance of Maintaining Your Drive For Long-Term Achievement
- ★ Methods for Keeping the Energy Levels Up and Preventing Burnout
- ★ Methods for Maintaining Accountability and Motivation

Realizing the Significance of Maintaining Your Drive for Long-Term Achievement

We go into detail on why it's crucial to maintain your drive over the long haul. Maintaining one's motivation is crucial to keeping one's forward momentum when working hard to achieve a goal, such as monetary success. The importance of retaining motivation and methods for doing so are discussed in this chapter.

The Importance of Maintaining Your Motivation and How to Do It

Inspiration is the fuel that keeps us going until we accomplish what we set out to do. When times are rough, it is what keeps us going. The road to financial success can be long and winding, so it's crucial to keep your spirits up along the way. Inevitably, there will be challenges and disappointments along the way as you work to amass wealth and achieve financial independence, which can take years.

We need to keep ourselves inspired to keep moving toward our goals. Motivated people are more likely to take the next step toward their goals and see their plans through to fruition. Because we are motivated by our goals, we are also more resilient in the face of adversity.

Motivating ourselves in this way also aids in keeping a constructive outlook. A person's ability to recognize and seize upon chances increases as his or her level of motivation rises. If we can keep a good attitude, which is often essential for triumphing over adversity, we'll have a far better chance of succeeding.

Methods for Maintaining Inspiration

Several methods exist for keeping oneself motivated, and each one may or may not be effective for a given individual. However, among the most successful methods are:

When we set challenging and feasible objectives, we are more likely to stick with them and remain motivated. If we want to see progress and keep the momentum going, we need to break down big goals into smaller, more attainable ones.

Rejoicing in accomplishments: Motivating yourself can be greatly aided by acknowledging and celebrating small victories along the road. It's important to stop and smell the roses when we accomplish something significant.

Imagining Victory: Maintaining motivation might be difficult, but visualizing success can be a great tool. Having a clear mental picture of our end goal might help us maintain our focus and drive while we work toward it.

Keeping ourselves surrounded by encouraging people: Staying motivated often requires the support of encouraging others. Spending time with encouraging loved ones is one option, as is exposing yourself to motivating media in the form of podcasts or videos.

Not Losing Steam

Successful people understand the importance of keeping the momentum going. Never give up on your dreams, no matter how many times you've been knocked down on the way to them. Keep the ball rolling by doing what can help:

We may keep ourselves focused and motivated by revisiting our goals frequently. It's crucial to keep in mind the reasons behind our goals and the outcomes we're shooting for.

We can see how far we've come and feel more accomplished if we keep tabs on our development. It can also show us where we're falling short so that we can change our approach.

Maintain your adaptability. Keeping your options open is key to keeping the momentum going. Along the way, we may need to make some course corrections or shift our focus, so we must remain flexible and receptive to new ideas and chances.

Breaks are necessary for keeping up momentum, so don't skip them. Taking a break to relax and rejuvenate will allow you to return to your goals with a clearer head and a greater sense of purpose.

In sum, maintaining your drive is crucial to your financial success. It's the engine that keeps us moving forward toward our objectives. Success in the financial realm can be maintained through the use of motivational techniques such as goal-setting, reward systems, mental imagery, and the company of like-minded people. Furthermore, it is essential to keep the ball rolling by periodically assessing our objectives, keeping scores of our progress, being adaptable, and taking breaks. We can build a comfortable living and secure financial future if we implement these plans.

Methods for Keeping the Energy Levels Up and Preventing Burnout

Long-term success requires persistent effort. Although a strong beginning is simple to achieve, maintaining that initial level of performance over time is far more difficult. Methods for maintaining enthusiasm and warding off burnout on the path to monetary independence are discussed in Chapter 9.

Establishing Reasonable Goals

To keep the momentum going, it's important to make sure your goals are reasonable. Thinking about your existing situation and the constraints you have is crucial when plotting out your goals. Your development will slow or stop altogether if your objectives are excessively ambitious. Nevertheless, if you set goals that you know you can accomplish in a manageable amount of time, you will be more likely to stick with your plan and remain inspired throughout the process.

Dissecting big goals into smaller, more achievable chunks is also crucial. Doing so will allow you to sketch out your course of action and track your progress more effectively. Acknowledging and rewarding your progress at key junctures will keep you motivated and feeling good about your progress so far.

How to Keep Your Eyes on the Prize

Keeping your eye on your motivations is another crucial tactic for keeping the momentum going. For what reasons do you seek material prosperity? Is it to support a family, to retire early, or to indulge a lifelong interest? Remembering your motivation will help you get through it when the going gets tough.

Whenever you ever feel like giving up, remind yourself of the reasons you got involved. Remembering your motivational "why" might help you stay committed to your long-term objectives.

The Importance of Putting Yourself First

Self-care is crucial for keeping your motivation up and preventing burnout. The inability to concentrate and stay motivated comes from ignoring your own physical and emotional requirements. Prevent this by making self-care a top priority, including getting plenty of sleep, eating right, and being active.

It's not just the body that has to be healthy to keep going; the mind does, too. Enjoy some downtime doing things that make you happy. Set aside time for things that improve your mental and emotional health, such as reading, listening to music, or spending time with loved ones.

Creating a Community of Helpers

One more way to keep going is to establish a network of people who have your back. Gather around you a group of people who will help you achieve your goals and give you honest feedback. You can get help and inspiration on your path to financial independence by joining a mastermind group or finding a mentor.

Remember that you will encounter obstacles and defeats along the way to your goal. Having someone you can count on for encouragement and support can help you keep going when things get tough.

Taking a Step Back to Reevaluate Progress

It's vital to check in on your financial objectives from time to time to see how you're doing against them. When you revisit your objectives, you may assess your progress, make course corrections as needed, and revel in your accomplishments.

The continued usefulness and compatibility of your goals with your long-term vision can be ensured by regular evaluation. Adjusting your objectives as life's curveballs come your way is a realistic possibility. You can make sure you're on the right path to financial success by evaluating your progress against your goals regularly.

To sum up, continuing with the same level of achievement is crucial if you want to be financially secure in the long run. To maintain motivation and avoid burnout, it is important to set reasonable objectives, remember your "why," prioritize self-care, build a support network, and periodically review and adjust your goals. You can keep moving forward toward your financial objectives if you use the methods discussed here.

Methods for Maintaining Accountability and Motivation

It can be difficult to keep up the level of effort and commitment necessary for long-term success on our own. As a result, it's important to have a network of people to lean on when times go tough.

Having people who believe in us and hold us accountable can boost our confidence and keep us moving forward toward our goals. Strategies for building a community of accountability and inspiration are discussed in this chapter.

Locate Your Backing System

Finding people who are willing to be there for you is the first step in creating a support network. Those could be members of your immediate or extended family, friends, coworkers, mentors, coaches, or even your online communities. Think about the upbeat, encouraging, and inspiring people in your life. These are the people who will provide you with the moral support and inspiration you require to keep going. Create a list of people who might help you achieve your goals and consider how they can hold you accountable and inspire you to keep going.

Share Your Expectations and Desires

The next stage is to let your support group know what you want and what you need from them. Give them an idea of the end goal and how they can contribute. Whether it's regular check-ins, accountability, or inspiration, be clear about what kind of help you need. Be specific about what you're hoping to gain from them, whether it's a sympathetic ear, helpful pointers, or a cheering section for your triumphs.

Prearrange Frequent Meetings

Frequent checks can be a powerful tool for maintaining accountability and inspiration. Meet with a trusted friend or mentor once a week or once a month to report on your progress and address any difficulties you're having. Take advantage of these gatherings to discuss what is and isn't working, as well as how to overcome any problems you may be experiencing. Having someone to check in with regularly is a great way to keep yourself on track and motivated when you're feeling down.

Join a Helping Organization

A great method to meet others who understand what you're going through is to join a support group. Certain difficulties, such as substance abuse, obesity, and professional advancement, might be addressed through specialized support groups. Find a community that shares your ideals and encourages you to grow personally and professionally. Having a community of people who care about you and want to see you succeed may be a tremendous boost to your will and determination.

Look for a Guide or a Coach.

Having a guide or coach to help keep you on track and motivated can be quite helpful. A mentor's knowledge and experience can be used to provide direction, advice, and encouragement. They can aid in self-analysis, pointing up improvement areas, and suggesting progress strategies. But, a coach can offer more organized help and keep you accountable by setting up scheduled meetings or check-ins. They are useful for establishing objectives, creating plans of action, and maintaining enthusiasm and concentration.

Honor Your Achievements

Lastly, remember to reward yourself for each milestone achievement. Recognizing your progress and rewarding yourself helps keep you going strong. Motivating feelings of success and fulfillment are another potential benefit. If you've recently gotten a promotion at work, reaching your savings goal, or finished a particularly difficult assignment, be sure to take some time to recognize and enjoy your accomplishments. If you want your friends and family to share in your joy, you need to let them in on your triumphs.

In conclusion, long-term success necessitates the establishment of a reliable system of checks and balances to ensure continued accountability and inspiration. Find your cheerleaders, tell them what you want and need help with, check in with them regularly, join a support group, get a coach or mentor, and enjoy the small victories along the way. You can accomplish your objectives and develop to your full potential with the help of encouraging people and outside forces.

Chapter 10

Bringing It All Together: The Millionaire Mindset Action Plan

Here, you'll find guidance on how to put the book's ideas into practice for real-world success. It lays out a methodical strategy for adopting a millionaire mentality and attaining financial independence, and it's packed with helpful advice and references for keeping your success on the rise.

Making a plan with a Millionaire Mindset is only the beginning of your journey to financial independence. To realize your dreams and amass the wealth you seek, it is essential to monitor your development and make necessary adjustments to your strategy. In this chapter, we'll go over the best practices for carrying out your plan of action, monitoring your development, and adjusting your strategy as needed.

★ Making a Game Plan to Achieve the Millionaire Mindset

★ Using Your Strategy for Achievement

★ Examining Your Development and Making Changes as Necessary

Making a Game Plan to Achieve the Millionaire Mindset

Establishing a Strategy for a Millionaire Mindset

In this book, we've covered a wide range of topics aimed at helping you think like a billionaire so that you can become one. Incorporate these practices into your everyday routine by making a strategy to implement them now. Developing your strategy for becoming a millionaire is the topic of this chapter.

In other words, set some objectives.

Establishing what it is you hope to achieve financially is the first step in developing a billionaire mindset. To do this, you must first determine your financial priorities, both now and in the future, and then map out a plan to get you where you want to be financial. Use the SMART goal-setting framework to ensure your objectives are SMART (specific, measurable, achievable, relevant, and time-bound).

Paying down credit card debt or saving for a home down payment are two possible examples of short-term financial goals. Possible long-term objectives include saving for retirement or launching your own business. Once you know what you want, you can divide the journey toward it into manageable daily, weekly, and monthly chunks.

Put together a budget

Once you know what you want to accomplish, you can start working on a financial strategy to get you there. The first step is to assess your financial standing by reviewing your income, expenditures, and other relevant data. Find ways to conserve money and reduce your spending, such as reducing your restaurant visits or refinancing your credit card interest rate.

Also, think about ways to boost your income, including getting a second job or starting your own business. Try to find safe places to put your money, like the stock market or a rental property. To reach your financial goals and adopt a millionaire mindset, it is essential that you first create a detailed financial plan.

Set up Routines

A millionaire's outlook is something that can be achieved slowly. It calls for persistent effort and the formation of routines that contribute to your financial objectives. Gratitude exercises, mental pictures of accomplishment, and periodic checks on your financial strategy can all help.

The same goes for prioritizing your health and fitness to maintain high levels of energy and focus, cultivating a morning routine that sets you up for a productive day, and practicing mindfulness and meditation to minimize stress and worry.

Find a Role Model

Learning from others who have already achieved financial success is one of the most efficient methods for adopting a millionaire mentality. If you want to learn more about investing, starting a business, or managing your own money, find a mentor who has done it before. A mentor can be a great source of advice, encouragement, and monitoring as you attempt to achieve your financial goals.

Networking with people who share your beliefs and aspirations by joining a mastermind group would be best. If you want to keep moving forward steadily toward your monetary objectives, surround yourself with people who believe in you and who encourage you.

Avoid Blaming Others

Last but not least, it is critical to hold yourself accountable by keeping tabs on your financial whereabouts. It entails keeping tabs on your financial situation, making necessary modifications, and rewarding yourself along the way.

To keep on track with your financial goals, consider getting guidance from a financial counselor or using financial planning software. Find an accountability partner or group to stay motivated and supported as you work towards your financial objectives.

In conclusion, if you want to become financially independent, you need to adopt the billionaire attitude and the behaviors of the wealthy. You may develop a millionaire mindset and achieve financial success by focusing on the following areas: goal setting, money management, daily routines, mentorship, and accountability. Always keep in mind that the ultimate goal of cultivating a millionaire mindset is not financial success per se, but rather the achievement of a life that is rich in experiences and freedom from constraints.

Using Your Strategy for Achievement

It's not enough to think like a billionaire; you also need to put the ideas from this book into practice. Making a plan that can be carried out is the subject of this chapter.

Establishing a Strategy for a Millionaire Mindset

As a first step in developing your millionaire mindset, read through all of the preceding chapters and pick out the tactics that will help you achieve your financial objectives. If you want to get things done, make a list of to-dos you know you can do in a given amount of time. Ensure that your objectives are

SMART (specific, measurable, attainable, relevant, and time-bound).

After compiling a list of things to do, arranging them in order of significance and urgency is wise. If you prioritize the most important tasks first, you are making headway toward your monetary objectives.

Keeping tabs on your development as you implement your plan is also crucial. You should measure your progress toward your goals by establishing milestones and deadlines for each action item. Doing this will make you more likely to maintain your drive and dedication to success.

Using Your Strategy for Achievement

With a plan in place, move forward with it. This is often the hardest part since it takes self-control and perseverance to keep going. A few tips to help you put your plan into action:

Create a schedule for yourself by which you will be more likely to follow through on your financial resolutions regularly. Dedicate a certain amount of time each day or week to completing your tasks, and try to keep to that timetable.

Get rid of anything that could potentially detract from your work or concentration on your goals. Figure out what is distracting you the most and do all you can to get rid of it. If you find yourself glued to your phone or computer, it might be time to cut back.

Keeping yourself motivated during the execution of your strategy is crucial. A good strategy to keep yourself motivated is to review your goals frequently. To keep yourself motivated on the path to financial independence, establish a vision board or write out your goals and display them where you will see them often.

Recognize Your Successes

Be sure to recognize and appreciate your progress, no matter how seemingly insignificant it may be. Gaining momentum and staying motivated is made easier when you take the time to recognize and appreciate your successes along the way. Recognize and appreciate your steps even if you have yet to arrive at your final destination.

Create mini-goals along the road and treat yourself when you reach them. There's no need to go all out for your rewards; something as simple as a movie night or a good meal can be just as motivating. You can increase your chances of success by rewarding yourself for short-term progress along the way.

Ultimately, it's crucial to be responsible for yourself and your objectives. You can achieve your goals by keeping close tabs on your development and revising your strategy regularly. It can be helpful to have someone to hold you accountable, such as a friend or family member, as you try to achieve your financial objectives.

In conclusion, it's crucial to adopt the mentality of a millionaire, but it's just as crucial to put that mentality into action and follow through with a strategy to reach your financial goals. You can cultivate the routines and outlook essential to financial success by making a plan and putting the ideas covered in the preceding chapters into action. Keep yourself inspired, focus on the task at hand, hold yourself accountable, and relish your successes. With these methods in place, you may build a life of prosperity and independence from your financial situation.

Examining Your Development and Making Changes as Necessary

If you want to succeed in anything, you need to keep tabs on your development and make course corrections as required. This is true in general, but it is more so when it comes to striving for material achievement and learning to think like a millionaire.

Many methods for forming the attitudes and routines that lead to material success have been discussed throughout this book. Yet, even the best-laid plans might fail if faced with surprises. To stay on course, it's important to keep tabs on your development and make modifications as needed.

These guidelines will help you keep tabs on your development and make the necessary adjustments to your strategy to guarantee your long-term success:

Develop Objective Goals and Criteria

Having well-defined goals and checkpoints along the road is essential for keeping tabs on your development. In this way, you may divide your long-term monetary objectives into shorter-term targets, which you can then work toward daily, weekly, and monthly.

If you want to save $50,000 in one year, you can save $1,000 weekly or $4,000 monthly as milestones along the way. You'll have something concrete to work toward, which will keep you motivated and focused.

Get on Track with the Help of Technology

There are many digital resources out there to assist you in monitoring your finances and achieving your objectives. Many solutions are available, from budgeting apps like Mint and You Need a Budget to investment tracking programs like Personal Capital and Betterment.

One option is to try out various resources until you find the ones that suit your needs best. The trick is to use technology to your advantage to keep on track and monitor your progress, whether that means a simple spreadsheet or more sophisticated software.

Consider Making Changes to Your Strategy Often

To ensure that you are making progress toward your financial objectives, it is crucial to evaluate your plan regularly and make any necessary adjustments. This may necessitate making adjustments to your financial plan, rethinking your approach to investing, or shifting how you plan to reach a certain goal.

Be adaptable and willing to make changes as necessary. There is no guarantee that a tactic that was successful in the past would remain so in the future. Staying on track and making headway toward your objectives can be ensured through regular plan reviews and tweaks.

Maintain Responsibility and Look for Help

Finally, while you try to achieve your financial goals, you must hold yourself accountable and enlist the help of others. You may stay motivated and on track by working with a financial coach or joining a mastermind group.

You might also tell your loved ones about your accomplishment or find a mentor who has already attained your desired degree of financial well-being. The most important thing is to figure out how to hold yourself accountable and keep yourself motivated no matter what strategy you end up using.

A necessary part of becoming financially successful and adopting a millionaire mindset is keeping tabs on your development and making necessary adjustments to your plan. Focus and determination may be maintained during the long road to financial independence by establishing reasonable goals, relying on tools to help you remain on track, checking in with yourself and others periodically, and making necessary adjustments. Keep in mind that becoming financially independent is a process that will take the rest of your life. But, if one adopts the proper frame of mind and implements the appropriate tactics, then anything is feasible.

Conclusion

To become financially independent and create the mindset of a millionaire, read The Millionaire Mindset: How to Think Like a Millionaire and Create a life you love. The author of this book urge readers to think positively, create specific, measurable, attainable, relevant, and timely (SMART) goals, push past their fears and doubts, and take action; readers are also advised to diversify their income, make smart financial investments, and cultivate an attitude of abundance.

This book provides concrete strategies, tips, and examples to help the reader better grasp and implement these principles. The book provides a straightforward, actionable method for doing everything from figuring out where money could be coming from to making a strategy and following it through.

One of the central lessons of this book is the importance of one's frame of mind in achieving material success. Success requires a positive outlook, and I shared methods for developing this outlook and overcoming the self-doubt and anxiety that can get in the way. Suppose readers take on a growth attitude and look for chances rather than problems. In that case, they will be able to alter their outlook and discover hitherto unimagined avenues for reaching their monetary objectives.

The concept of SMART objectives is emphasized, which is another important takeaway from the book. Readers can sharpen their focus and avoid distractions by developing a plan with SMART objectives. The book teaches readers to establish SMART goals for monetary success and includes methods for monitoring and revising the plan as needed.

The necessity of getting started and keeping the momentum going toward one's financial goals is also emphasized throughout this book. Creating forward momentum toward one's financial goals is possible when one adopts practices that support them, such as budgeting, saving, and investing. Building a support network and practicing thankfulness for one's blessings are just two of the many tangible methods for gaining momentum and maintaining motivation that is outlined in this book.

This book also provides useful guidance on diversifying your income and making smart investments to amass wealth. Readers may boost their income and accumulate wealth over time by recognizing income opportunities and investing in assets that produce passive income. The book instructs readers on recognizing investment opportunities, controlling risk, and constructing a diversified portfolio to assist readers in attaining financial independence.

If you want to learn the habits of the wealthy and what it takes to become financially independent, "The Millionaire Mindset: How to Think Like a Millionaire and Achieve Financial Freedom" is an excellent book to read. This book provides useful techniques, suggestions, and insights for anyone at any stage of their financial journey, from those just starting to those who want to take their financial game to the next level. Successful people have the appropriate mentality and habits, and they take regular action in the direction of their goals.

About the Author

O.G. CEO, is an established business leader and a seasoned financial expert. O.G. CEO has established herself as an innovative leader who motivates her employees and those around her to pursue their dreams of financial independence. Success in the cutthroat business world and her strategies for achieving it are discussed. She has been instrumental in the growth and prosperity of countless people and organizations.

Besides being a highly successful businesswoman, O.G. CEO is an outspoken supporter of increasing women's access to financial education and tools. No matter one's origin, gender, or current situation, she thinks everyone can become financially independent and build the life they want.